Before the Forest Burns

Poems & Translations

Before the Forest Burns

Poems & Translations by

Leslie Monsour

© 2025 Leslie Monsour. All rights reserved.
This material may not be reproduced in any form, published,
reprinted, recorded, performed, broadcast,
rewritten, or redistributed without
the explicit permission of Leslie Monsour.
All such actions are strictly prohibited by law.

Cover design by Shay Culligan
Cover art by Linda Saccoccio
Author photo by Leslie Monsour

ISBN: 978-1-63980-791-8
Library of Congress Control Number: 2025938448

Kelsay Books
502 South 1040 East, A-119
American Fork, Utah 84003
Kelsaybooks.com

to my family

Acknowledgments

Poems in this book have appeared (some in slightly different versions) in the following print and online publications:

Able Muse: "In Such a Place," "That's Why There Are So Many"
Alabama Literary Review: "The Sloth," "White Christmas," "Doggedness"
The Alarming Beauty of the Sky: "On Finding a Salamander in the Hollywood Hills," "Desert Prayer"
American Arts Quarterly: "*Clair de Lune*"
Cadenza: "Lovers and Spiders"
The Chimaera: "'When the Swallows Come Back to Capistrano,'" "Soldier on the Plane," "At the Summer Poetry Festival"
The Dark Horse: "Palm Springs Desert Dystopia," "Web," "Hemingway's Poetic Flair"
First Things: "*Olea Europaea*," "The Lesson of the Artichoke"
Galway Review: "Herd at Ballyvaughan," "The Fifth Horseman," "Stella and Her Bone"
Indelibility: "*Showboat* Revival"
Judd's Hill Winery: "Winegrowers' Song"
Light: "On Misreading a Wine Ad," "Satan's Garden," "Henny Youngman at the Garden of Eden," "'The opening line must have urgency,'" "Colorless, Odorless, Tasteless," "Geosociology," "Two Complaints," "Riddle"
Literary Matters: "Clockwork Ravens"
Love Affairs at the Villa Nelle: "Coming to Terms over Coffee"
Measure: "Laurel Canyon," "The House Sitter"
Mezzo Cammin: "September Night," "May Nasturtiums," "Polishing off the Sherry"
Mrs. Nelson's Class: "Diablo"
Nimrod: "The Ultimate Riddle"
The Orchards Poetry Journal: "Life on the Los Angeles River"
Pratik: "Sierra Nevada Chasm, Tioga Pass"

The Raintown Review: "'Brightening as They Fail,'" "Happy Hour"
The Rotary Dial: "Summer Again," "Forbidding Fruit"
String Poet: "Sor Juana Inés de la Cruz—Five Sonnets," "'I'll Catch a Ride'"

Contents

Summer Again	15

I.

On Finding a Salamander in the Hollywood Hills	19
Sierra Nevada Chasm, Tioga Pass	20
Palm Springs Desert Dystopia	21
Desert Prayer	22
In Such a Place	23
Hollywood Sidewalk Tankas	24
"When the Swallows Come Back to Capistrano"	25
Laurel Canyon	26
Life on the Los Angeles River	29
Winegrowers' Song	30
September Night	31
Herd at Ballyvaughan	32
The Sloth	34
Web	36
The Fifth Horseman	37
Clockwork Ravens	40
That's Why There Are So Many	41

II.

On Misreading a Wine Ad	45
A Take on Emily Dickinson: Polishing Off the Sherry	46
Another Take: Heartburn denotes that Dinner was	47
Showboat Revival	48
Hemingway's Poetic Flair	49
Satan's Garden	50
Henny Youngman at the Garden of Eden	51

Lovers and Spiders	52
To My Gracious (Absent) Hosts	53
Parental Misguidance	54
Fire and Ice and Wind	55
"The opening line must have urgency."	56
A Five-Year-Old Explains the Health Food Store	57
Colorless, Odorless, Tasteless	58
Geosociology	59
Two Complaints	60
At the Summer Poetry Festival	61
Coming to Terms over Coffee	62
Vers de Société à la Pandémie	63

III.

Sor Juana Inés de la Cruz: Five Sonnets	67
#149	68
#151	69
#152	70
#175	71
#176	72
The Ultimate Riddle	73

IV.

Diablo	77
"I'll Catch a Ride"	83
Stella and Her Bone	85
A Quiet Evening at Home	86
Don't Speak to Me of Joy	87
Soldier on the Plane	88

V.

Autobiographical	91
The Rose in the Center of the Room—A Wedding Toast	92
"I Almost Just Woke Up"	93
May Nasturtiums	94
Olea Europaea	95
The Lesson of the Artichoke	96
"Brightening As They Fail"	97
Forbidding Fruit	98
White Christmas	99
Happy Hour	101
In Memoriam	102
The House Sitter	103
Clair de Lune	104
Doggedness	105
Riddle	106
Notes	109

Summer Again

The ink-drop bumblebee invades
    The squashes, bloom by bloom,
Amid the beans that weave in braids
    And dangle from their loom.

The lizard, livening its bones,
    Pretends that it can print
Its belly on the blazing stones
    Beside the cooling mint,

Where cabbage butterflies perform
    A papery ballet
And dodge the garden hose's warm,
    Rainbow-illumined spray.

The scene, familiar and brief,
    Age after age returns—
As green returns to summer leaf,
    Before the forest burns.

I.

On Finding a Salamander in the Hollywood Hills

Into deep shade a salamander crept.
It curled its body there and moistly slept,
Till I removed an old agave pot.

The mire convulsed in little specks of blue.
A shape was generated from the stew,
As if the mud had conjured up a thought.

I scooped it up and cupped it in my palm.
It flashed its bolting tongue, stayed boldly calm,
Its aspic flesh congealing in a knot

Of ancient blood, the ripened afterbirth
Of roses, springing from the fabled earth,
Preposterous, like something time forgot.

Across the laurel chaparral and oak,
The shadows shrank, the season smelled of smoke.
The salamander, so the myth is taught,

Can withstand fire. With fierce, bituminous stare,
The way a dying star dims with a flare,
It blinked away the noonday sun's white-hot

And airy universe of bees and birds
And poets prospering on weightless words,
Then slid back to its ponderous realm of rot
And clammy slumber in this land of drought.

Sierra Nevada Chasm, Tioga Pass

    For C. Doe

If you stare inside
The gorge to contemplate its
Breathtaking divide

Your senses leave you.
The distant rush of snowmelt
Is just a preview

Of the granite chute
Whose mighty exhalation
Lets nothing take root,

Or even tarry
Slightly. The force is ruthless
And necessary.

You might want to stand
Still, feel your self erased, then
Turn back to soft land,

Begin to regain
Your senses, smell pine, feel sun,
Hear birdsong again.

Palm Springs Desert Dystopia

Now is the hour the desert moon grows bright
And floats above the mountains, while its fool
Twin hides in lights that light the swimming pool,
And landscape boulders bake throughout the night,
Lit like stage props with floods of gold and pink.
The desert's hardly desert anymore:
The surest thing to come by is a drink,
And sand mostly affects a golfing score.

The Sinaloan pool man, after rain,
Finds drowned tarantulas around the drain.
He scoops them in his net and then forgets
He left them in the morning sun to dry.
After he's gone, the clumps revivify
And scatter like anarchic marionettes.

Desert Prayer

Prayer is the contemplation of the facts
of life from the highest point of view.
                    —Emerson

A gleaming granite ocean, bold as light
and strewn with bright, coarse stuff—a million suns,
the shells of ancient seas and modern guns—
the grand Mojave disappears at night,

its long and open syllable of air,
the breath of all that lives and dies out there.

Surrounded by the silent sprawl of sage,
I see the stark indifference of its grace,
the glare of stillness on its living face;
I feel the hope-free weight of rockbound age

and, for an instant, heaven-reaching joy,
at poppies pushing through the wind-cracked clay.

The sudden dive when hawk and eagle soar
is sky's collaboration with the land.
Here, eye-like burrows, socketed in sand,
surrender truth from earth's consenting floor;

here, timorous hearts keep time in fur and bone.
I know the beat; their thumping is my own.

In Such a Place

I'm killing minutes in a city park,
Reflecting while the sky turns overcast.
Strange how the orderly, unblemished grounds
Appear to have no vestige of the past.

The parking meters accept credit cards.
The shrubbery is plain and well-behaved.
Two ravens poke the lawn half-heartedly.
The spaces in between the grass are paved.

Birdsong is banished by the leaf blowers
and power mowers edging ficus trunks.
The gas fumes are the only vagrants here,
Loitering in the air like drowsy drunks.

A man who walks a Yorkie on a leash
Pauses to let the tiny dog complete
Its tiny crap, dispatched with plastic bag
And carried to a bin across the street.

There's no dead branch in sight, no memory,
No process of decay, nothing to burn.
Where nothing rots, nothing surprising lives.
In such a place, what more is there to learn?

Hollywood Sidewalk Tankas

Dark Tourism

On North Hayworth Street
No one exits the tour van
For sidewalk selfies
In front of the apartment
Where F. Scott Fitzgerald died.

Eye of the Beholder

The spattered sidewalk
At Selma and Cherokee
Is sparrows' artwork—
Abstract Expressionism—
Something for the Broad, downtown.

Sheltered

Walk around the pile
Gently. Try not to disturb
The cardboard and tarps.
A person has built a home
Shaped like a Tongva dwelling.

Scientology Group Acquires Art Deco Cedars of Lebanon Hospital

Sidewalk guards patrol
The strange, lusterless blue 'church'
Where I first breathed air.
The windows reflect nothing.
Even the sky looks opaque.

"When the Swallows Come Back to Capistrano"

Popular song by Leon René, 1939

It's easy to forget what brought them here,
since those ideal conditions pre-exist us;
but still it's fun pretending every year.

In fact, the feathered migrants go unmissed, as
long as the fiestas and parades go on,
as heartwarming and bankable as Christmas.

Lagoons with mud for nest-building are gone,
paved over for itinerants in cars;
but almost any bird that soars at dawn

will pass for those once-faithful comeback stars.
The mission bells are loud and punctual.
The mariachi trumpets and guitars

assault the loudspeakers as usual,
and Aztec dancers with their drummers follow.
The first graders perform in whimsical

felt beaks and wings, "Good Morning, Mr. Swallow."
Then comes the old hit song beloved by all,
whose chorus of return, however hollow,

must, at all cost, be sung each spring and fall.
Nostalgia holds humanity in thrall.
A man-made mud nest clings to the north wall.

Laurel Canyon

Mid-winter, we approach the often fog-draped
inclines of laurel and black walnut trees.
Along the way, we pass the fizz and wheeze
of sprinklers dousing fertilized and landscaped

plots filled with nursery imports from the Valley,
before we reach the verge of chaparral
and open space where I can throw the ball
for Mick, the energetic border collie.

Sometimes there is a gardener coming down
the driveway of a lofty residence,
and farther up, a parked Mercedes Benz
looks newly washed. The dog will romp and clown,

retrieving the hurled ball and panting hard.
The groundskeeper nods amiably, then heaves
his bulky bag of branches and wet leaves
into the bin and climbs back toward the yard.

In early spring, a swift, seed-herding gust
drives clatterings of casings down the lane,
and haloed pods drift down in weightless rain,
mandorla-shaped, to settle in the dust.

They're not unlike the radiant termite surge
that clots and showers from some rotted sill.
The loosened wings fall whirling in a veil,
as black flies whine a dead coyote's dirge.

The stillness is incongruous and sheer:
some quail disperse above the prickly pear,
their whirring wings like chuffings of a mare;
a neighbor tries her cell phone in the clear.

The hill's a sea of roiling, tossing grass,
and Mick sometimes will lose the ball in dense
new growth, or over some low redwood fence.
Sun pours through still-bare branches as we pass

and head back to the provinces of noise,
forsaking pensive space and native brush,
the redtail's cry ascending in the hush,
for leaf blower-enforced suburban poise.

By June, the elm trees are no longer bare.
Where winter light reached down and kindly made
us warm, now spreads a canopy of shade.
Today we find the fire inspectors there.

The grasses that had drifted with each puff
are motionless, a dried-out weary thatch
that crackles underfoot. Mick leaves the patch
with burrs and foxtails buried in his ruff.

The dangerous acres rule themselves, until
a summer day when trucks appear and bring
a team of men whose steel machetes ring
above the chainsaws droning from the hill,

which now stands shaved, becalmed, the workers gone.
The upper slope seems even more remote.
The mockingbird has quieted its throat;
the Nuttall and the scrub jay have withdrawn.

And when September's silent swelter falls,
the yucca stalks have blackened and expired;
the hummingbirds have soberly retired
from weeks of wild agave bacchanals

to suck from homely tree tobacco thimbles.
November first (it rained the previous night),
a film crew comes to choreograph a fight.
Two swordsmen thrust and parry phallic symbols.

I hold Mick back, the mud caked to his paws.
We stand aside and watch the fencing actors
against a background of wet, shiny cactus,
while dripping live oaks shudder in applause.

In late December, we have early suns.
Surveyors have set up a tripod stand—
investment groups are buying up the land.
From sycamores, hawks cock their eyes like guns.

Life on the Los Angeles River

A heron stops in early spring
At an unlikely place,
Wading on stilts with folded wing
And skeptical, cool grace,

Aiming its handsome banded eye,
Its sleek, extended beak,
At darting schools of minnow fry
Inhabiting the creek

And slurry that the storm drains pour
Into the concrete flood
Canal, whose excavated floor
Has been returned to mud.

New sandbars bring forth willow shrubs,
And recent marshes hum
With frogs that feed on insect grubs;
Now water birds have come.

Today we watch the heron fly.
Its magnitude and hue
Reveal at once the reason why
We call it great and blue.

Winegrowers' Song

Ignoring what our mothers used to teach,
We taste the dirt—not only taste, but savor
The subtle, sandy clay and loamy flavor
Of Napa Valley soil that spreads its reach

Of live oak and bay laurel to the sill
Of the Pacific, where chill fogs ascend.
Pinot and Chardonnay best comprehend
The climate whispered here. The sky is still

Above the Silverado Trail. The river
Inhales the musky air and rests its powers
Awhile. In May the slopes are quiet bowers
Of tiny, faint, sweet blooms, their tender shiver

Commencing the one-hundred-days' surprise
Of ripening, unriddled mysteries,
As vines interpret *terra's* reveries
Into a song all tongues can recognize.

September Night

Moonlit, a nimble spider weaves.
Low creatures stir in every shadow:
Full cricket choir, wild clash of leaves,
A tree rat drops an avocado.

Beyond earth's mild nocturnal din
Persists an ever-present drone
Of less primeval origin:
The traffic on the 101.

The King's Road, El Camino Real,
The highway of the mission bell,
For centuries an oxcart trail
From San Diego to Carmel

Now issues white noise everywhere:
The rush of latex on cement,
The eruption of combusted air,
The roar of miles-per-gallon spent.

It reaches canyons miles away,
Where white moths fly into the moon,
As owls swoop low after their prey,
And summer will be over soon.

Herd at Ballyvaughan

For Nicholas

The silence was superb at summer's end;
The crows were elsewhere on the sunny bay;
The pasture and the hills, a greeny blend
Of grasses in the stillness of midday.

The cattle in the center of the field
Were all that could be heard, their tug and munch
A syncopated chant of herbal yield,
Their universe a pasture bright with lunch.

The quiet rhythm of the afternoon
Could almost put the whole world in a trance;
Thus, it occurred to me to hum a tune
As I stood yards away outside the fence.

The curly-coated Galloways, young steers
Brought up for beef, lifted their faces one
By one, bright yellow tags pinned to their ears,
And listened, moving towards me in the sun.

I thought of Helios's sacred cattle,
The foolish sailors on a killing spree;
I heard the lapping tide where puffins paddle
And thought about the isle at Innisfree.

And then I sang the "Song of Wandering Aengus,"
The Angus, kin to Galway's curly-coat,
And Yeats the poet who wrote about and sang us
Tales of mystic Celtic anecdote.

Today, I summon Yeats's *deep heart's core,*
The peaceful herd at Galway's glassy bay,
Come, grace the groves of oak and sycamore
In these dry hills five thousand miles away.

The Sloth

The mugginess had soaked us to our skin.
The man who brought the rental car was rude
And spoke a lazy Spanish with a grin.
We set out in a dilatory mood.

Our talk was idle: "I don't care . . ." "Perhaps . . ."
"Could you turn up the air conditioning?"
We swayed and bumped along, comparing maps
And routes, or drowsily envisioning

The might-have-beens of old or failed affairs,
Occasionally nodding off in twisting,
Ascending, and descending scenic lairs
With sudden rivers frothing through the misting

Volcanic chasms, glimpsed through missing planks
Of rusted, narrow, questionable bridges.
We passed the wild impatiens on the banks
Of moss along the road, the crimson ridges,

Tobacco-ruled, till something up ahead
Made us slam on the brakes. We met a sloth,
Unfairly named, midway, in arduous tread,
Its shabby shape, a hunk of burlap cloth

That groped the yellow line, the halfway point
Of where it had to go. Its chances poor,
It labored forward like a battered saint
Expecting pain, determined to ignore

The perils and the treachery of asphalt
And humans, heir to an instinctive code,
As several drivers coasted to a halt,
Intrigued by the enigma in the road.

Doors swinging open, iPhone shutters snapping,
The eager paparazzi of the cloud
Forest emerged to marvel, almost clapping
At every inch of progress, sharing aloud

Their knowledge and surprise, advancing near
And commenting: "The two-toed ones attack."
"Moths feed on algae growing in its fur."
"It carries ecosystems on its back."

The sloth, with solemn resolution, gained
The other side—the grasses and the grove
Of palms and rubber trees—while we remained
Outside our cars and watched the branches move.

Web

After "Design" by Robert Frost

A black and yellow garden spider toils
In counterclockwise interstitial coils
To join the cartwheel radii of its snare
Then occupies the hub and hangs midair.

What forces have inspired it to resemble
A flower blossoming whose petals tremble
In noon's light breezes, fooling butterflies?
The lie turns into truth before my eyes.

But let's be fair. The spider's masquerade
Must not be misconstrued as wrong or bad;
Nor should the trussed, convulsing copperwing
Be seen as innocent or suffering.
Darwin explains it better than The Fall:
Nature selects. It's hard to watch, that's all.

The Fifth Horseman

Some one prepared this mighty show
To which without a Ticket go
The nations and the Days—
               —Emily Dickinson

I once owned a tropical pony
Of Peruvian Paso descent
Bred from those brought by murderous Pizarro
To plunder the continent.

The bloodline continued and flourished,
Evolving in fair replica
As a bush horse bred mostly for pleasure
Throughout Central America.

The stable hand's name was Edwin.
A machete hung at his side.
He cleared out the trail every morning
Before others went out for a ride.

Overnight, the golden silk spiders
Spun orb webs a meter wide.
I never rode into the forest
Without Edwin before me as guide.

"At night dey catch ratbat and owl, mon,"
He'd say, as we rode through the trees,
Slicing silk with his rusted machete.
"In Jamaica, mon, plenty of dees."

The place was too sultry for saddles—
We used nothing but bridle and bit—
Not a pad or a blanket, just horse sweat
And welts; I was soon used to it.

Early morning, the horses were freshest—
They'd leap over culvert and log,
As the canopy woke with the racket
Of capuchin, parrot, and frog.

Now and then, we caught sight of the quetzal,
The blending iguana and viper,
And every Nymphalidae butterfly
Of sapphire, ruby, and copper.

On the floor of the soft-wood forest
Pink ginger bloomed in the mud
And the path sometimes sank like a quicksand,
Under puddles from yesterday's flood.

But our sure-footed ponies were savvy,
Stepping lightly and circling around
On a carpet of fern bed and grasses,
While avoiding the fire ant's mound,

Where anteaters dig for their breakfast,
Immune to the stinging attacks.
Then the trail reached the stream, and the horses
Would swim us across on their backs,

With Edwin on guard for the caimans
That lurk on the shore or afloat,
While the sloth sleeps on high in the branches,
And the moths lay their eggs in her coat.

There, she dreams of the end of her species
To the hum of the stingless bees,
As they sing to the dwindling forest
How the cast has been cut with the trees—

For the house has exceeded capacity,
And the show's not so mighty these days:
Unlike the great God of the empires,
Nature works in well-understood ways.

The prophet who wrote of the horsemen—
Death, Pestilence, Famine, and War—
Unknowingly left out the fifth one:
Mass Extinction surpasses all four.

He's been picking up speed at full gallop
After sixty-or-so million years.
Neither Edwin nor I could foresee it,
When we rode there like two pioneers

On our Panamanian ponies
Of Peruvian Paso descent
Bred from those brought by murderous Pizarro
To plunder the continent.

Clockwork Ravens

The heat wave brings euphoria to some:
With no desire to hibernate, the lizard
Poised keen and energized, flashes his scissored
Tongue to assess the climate's strange perfume.
Two yellow butterflies are being wed
And climb a shaft of sun to celebrate
The sudden opportunity to mate.
The jack-o-lantern teems with overfed
Fruit flies and sweaty mold, rotting with glee.
I pour a glass of iced verbena tea
Cut from the fragrant sprigs along the wall.
It feels more like midsummer than mid-fall.

Is this euphoria or a state of shock?
The seasons grow increasingly remote,
And time has long run out for idle talk.
Hear how the ravens read between the lines,
Croaking and chuckling in the dying pines.
Some call them crows, but these are raven birds
With grave vocabularies, cryptic words,
Uncanny acrobatics of the throat.
Curiously, they mimic what they mock:
The long-lost sound of winding up a clock.

That's Why There Are So Many

A soft, black plum released itself
        From all its branch-held kin;
It landed with a single *klop*
        And opened up its skin.

The narrow slit showed amber flesh
        Of glistening surprise,
Which, uncontained, spilled drop by drop,
        Inviting in the flies.

But all of nature's laws and forces,
        Including gravity,
Were not enough to keep it there
        To grow into a tree;

For I was there to see the fruit
        Split open at my feet,
Inviting me before the flies
        To taste its sun-warmed meat.

I took it to the kitchen sink
        That idle, blind-hot day,
And rinsed it well and ate it clean,
        Then threw the stone away.

II.

On Misreading a Wine Ad

Made to go with the foods you love

The fools I love drink any old wine,
Whether red, rosé, or white.
A wine made to go with these chums of mine
Should flow freely and last all night.

The wine that is made for the fools I adore,
Yours truly included, I fear,
Is the wine that says "Yes" to the clamor for more;
Its abundance is what we hold dear.

As long as there's plenty when push comes to shove,
From late afternoon until dawn,
Any wine's made to go with the fools I love,
As long as the wine's never gone.

A Take on Emily Dickinson: Polishing Off the Sherry

. . . my eyes, like the Sherry in the Glass, that the Guest leaves

The glass I leave's an empty one;
I polish off each drop.
It's only when the bottle's done
that I know when to stop.

Were I a Homestead guest on those
nights of superb surprise,
I'd kill the means by which she chose
to acquaint us with her eyes.

Another Take: Heartburn denotes that Dinner was

Ashes denote that Fire was
  —Emily Dickinson

Heartburn denotes that dinner was—
Salute the Secret Sauce
For the Kentucky Colonel's sake
And every franchise boss—

Vittles exist the first in Farms
Then Processes occur—
How Flavors are achieved, only
The Chemist knows for sure.

Showboat Revival

> *Fish got to swim and birds got to fly,*
> *I got to love one man till I die . . .*
>   —Oscar Hammerstein

Fish got to fly, and birds got to swim,
I was married to her, now I'm married to him.

Hemingway's Poetic Flair

> *If I feel physically as if the top of my head were taken off,*
> *I know that is poetry.*
> —Martha Dickinson Bianchi, *Life and Letters of Emily Dickinson*

When Ernest Hemingway awoke at dawn before his wife,
He crept downstairs and wrote the greatest poem of his life.

Satan's Garden

> With apologies to Dorothy
> Frances Gurney

Black aphids, white flies do my yard in;
Rats and gophers leave little of worth.
I'm nearer to hell in my garden
Than anywhere else on earth.

Henny Youngman at the Garden of Eden

He knows he's bombing when the lion snores,
Hyenas hiss, and birds fall from the trees;
But then he hits a funny bone and scores
With his immortal "Take my rib . . . please."

Lovers and Spiders

The spider is a ruthless one;
But lovers, too, behave like this,
For I have seen a fly undone
After a long and hungry kiss.

To My Gracious (Absent) Hosts

> For Caroline and Michel, New York City, May 30, 2015
> (After William Carlos Williams)

I gorged on cherries from the fridge;
I gazed o'er city, water, bridge;
I poured some whiskey in my glass,
And gratefully I parked my ass.

Parental Misguidance

We don't choose disillusionment;
Our parents do that for us.
They hope to make us soloists,
When we should join the chorus.

Fire and Ice and Wind

Frost knew enough of hatred and desire
To say the world would end in ice or fire;
But I have seen enough stupidity
To say that wind's the greater enemy.

"The opening line must have urgency."

—A workshop instructor

Shall I compare thee to a summer's day?
Not now, I've really got to run.
Then here's some urgency to make you stay:
Your zip's undone.

A Five-Year-Old Explains the Health Food Store

The hell food store is where they sell
The stuff that keeps us feeling well
Like mushroom juice and ox blood gel
And other stuff that comes from hell.

Colorless, Odorless, Tasteless

The term "inert" applies to noble gases.
It's also aptly said of noble classes.

Geosociology

When two tectonic plates collide,
They either buckle, or there is subduction.
The same is true of egos: one side
Goes under, or they each suffer reduction.

Two Complaints

In a Nutshell

Be wary when you hear, "Long story short."
It means you're going to get the full report.

Let Sleeping Dogs Lay

> Remember that even though many people do use lay for lie,
> others will judge you unfavorably if you do.
> —Merriam Webster's Collegiate Dictionary

Why is it no one lies down anymore?
They're always laying in their hammocks or
Their beds. You don't see pigs lay in their pens,
Do you? They leave the laying to the hens.

At the Summer Poetry Festival

Ah there she is, all siren-like and fair,
Looking for blurbs, no doubt. I like her hair.
As for the manuscript she's bandying,
I've heard it's so-so, but I'll praise the thing.
My Pulitzer and sultry, southern lilt
Routinely do the trick—she'll all but wilt
Into my arms. I see she wears a ring.
So much the easier to have a fling.

She's caught my gaze. I'll raise my glass and wink.
What luck, she has my book and wants a drink.
I'll meet her at the bar. *What have we here?*
Sign it for you? With pleasure, yes, my dear.
No pen? No matter. Later on we'll go
And look for one inside my bungalow.

Coming to Terms over Coffee

I'd never fall in love with you.
Love fizzles out and mortifies.
Affection's fine, and it will do.

Besides, love's common as bamboo
And flits about like butterflies.
How could I fall in love with you

And send you flowery billets-doux
Or hit upon you otherwise?
Affection's fine, and it will do.

Lovers are fickle and untrue;
They tell each other little lies.
I'd never fall in love with you,

Stoop to some secret rendezvous,
And be reduced to quivering sighs:
Affection's fine, and it will do.

So pour your famous foreign brew,
As dark and jolting as your eyes.
I'll never fall in love with you;
Affection's fine, and it will do.

Vers de Société à la Pandémie

   After Philip Larkin

My nitwit neighbor who lives down the street
And can't tell seven inches from six feet,

Came jogging by and caught me unaware
While checking mail, and asked me if I'd care

To join her later outside on her deck
For wine. I felt her breathing down my neck

And quickly backed away. "It's BYO,"
She chirped. I faltered. "Gee, Liz, I don't know."

"Come on," she said. "We all could use some wine."
Oh, god, thought I, she's like a porcupine,

Too close for comfort, also too insistent.
These days, I've grown increasingly resistant

To small talk, corny punch lines, followed by
Infectious phony laughter and a sigh.

I stared at her and wondered, what could she
Want with a cynical old shit like me?

But, still, I have a brand new linen blouse.
Am I to simply wear it around the house?

No ball games on TV. They've closed the beach.
I hardly even dare to eat a peach

Or part my hair. Perhaps I'll bring a flask
Of Scottish drink to swig beneath my mask;

And single malt does ever so much more
Than Chardonnay to turn a crashing bore

Into a scintillating, vibrant wit.
Nah, it's a waste of time. Get out of it.

Besides, I'm happier staying safe at home
Watching the evening news or reading some

Old issue of *The Saturday Review*
And staring out the window, as a few

Old dried-up bougainvillea blossoms drift
In silence, as the evening breezes shift,

And nightfall drains the color from the day . . .
Oh, hell, then. "Sure, Liz, what time did you say?"

III.

Sor Juana Inés de la Cruz: Five Sonnets

Sor (Sister) Juana Inés de la Cruz (1648–1695) is universally regarded as the first major poet of the Americas and the intellectual mother of Mexico. Because her works rose like a flame from the ashes of religious disapproval, the embattled writer came to be identified with the magical bird of myth, the Phoenix. With the publication of her first book, Sor Juana was also dubbed *Musa décima,* "Tenth Muse," an epithet of praise originally applied to Sappho and shared by Sor Juana's New England contemporary, Anne Bradstreet.

At twenty or twenty-one years of age, having lived in the court of the Viceroy since the age of fifteen, Juana Inés changed her life dramatically. She ceased to be Juana Ramírez de Asbaje and became Sor Juana Inés de la Cruz when she joined the Convent of the Barefoot Carmelites in 1669. There is meager documentation of her years of courtly life. Only speculation can answer why she chose to leave its aristocratic comforts and the avid admirers that surrounded her. It may have been to evade the growing expectations that she, as a desirable, popular young woman, should be married; but married life was a condition she desperately wished to avoid, in order to devote herself to the life of the mind. Convent living presented a logical, if not ideal, alternative.

#149

*Out of spirited resentment, she assesses
the choice of a state that lasts until death*

To contemplate the perils of the sea
Would end all voyages. If made aware
Of all potential dangers, none would dare
Challenge the bull's defiant bravery.

No skilled equestrian, if he could see
His bold, unbridled stallion or mare
At full force, charging down the thoroughfare,
Would hope to harness such fierce energy.

While one who has enough intrepid nerve
To shrug off risk and seek Apollo's lair,
Emboldened by an urge to govern fate,

Will steer the sun-bathed rig beyond earth's curve
And try it all, be all, go everywhere,
Not shrink into a safe and stagnant state.

#151

She suspects disguised cruelty in the comfort Hope brings

Unending ailment, Hope, your curse abides;
and I've remained enthralled year after year.
In equal measurements of faith and fear,
your scales forever balance both their sides,

forever hold their teasing, teetering lull.
But at the verge of tipping, your deceit
allows no mounting or decrease in weight,
giving despair and promise equal pull.

Who stripped you of your true name, murderer?
Essentially, yours is a greater crime:
you dally with the soul, suspending her

between two fortunes, wretched and sublime—
not so that life will linger or endure,
rather to let fate take its own sweet time.

#152

Rosy obsession

Rosy obsession of humanity,
intricate dreams all daydreamers pursue,
and all vain dreams of treasure's golden hue,
demented Hope, gilded insanity,

world without end, springlike longevity,
feeble imaginings of verdant dew,
the now that comes to the successful few,
the never of the jinxed majority:

they chase your night in search of your pink dawn
who fit their spectacles with rosy lies
and color things as they would have them be;

while I know better what my fate will spawn,
and in each hand I hold each of my eyes,
and touch only what I can plainly see.

#175

Absence does more harm than jealousy

The jilted and the jealous suffer much:
the former with despair, the latter, spleen.
The jealous one imagines the unseen;
the other feels reality's cold touch.

The jealous one enjoys his frenzied ire,
consumed in vengeful and possessive fever.
The one who is forsaken pines forever
and can't escape the ache of his desire.

The jealous one dreams of elimination;
the lonely one loses all hope of sleep.
The jealous one trades blame for indignation;

bereft, the castaway can only weep.
So, when it comes to woe, it's desolation,
not green-eyed spite, whose wound is felt most deep.

#176

Loving without chagrin

I can't hold on to you, nor can I quit,
nor know why, whether out of reach or near you,
a certain something happens to endear you,
while other somethings urge me to forget.

Since you will not release me or reform,
with luck, I'll moderate my heart somewhat,
so half recoils when you invade my thought,
and half is tender, amorous, and warm.

There's hope if this suffices as affection,
for quarrelling is but a way to die,
and jealousy brings nothing but the worst.

Who offers half, denies a whole connection,
so while you're out there practicing your lie,
know that my devastation's well-rehearsed.

The Ultimate Riddle

From riddles contained in La Galatea, A Pastoral Romance *by Miguel de Cervantes Saavedra, in loving memory of Kate Light*

    She is obscure and yet she's clear;
still, ambiguities abound.
She keeps her truths from being found,
but, in the end, her truths appear.
She is at times the child of wit,
at others, sired by fantasy;
she's known to breed great rivalry,
though she bestows no benefit.

    All are familiar with her name,
including tykes of youngest age.
Scholars and masters each engage
their keenest powers to guess her aim,
and there's no crone who won't accept
an invitation from this dame
to pass the hours in pleasant game
and prove her match or prove inept.

    Philosophers burn midnight oil
her cryptic data to explain;
the more bewildered they remain,
the harder still she makes them toil.
A bumptious brat, a teasing quiz,
a brazen vamp at bothering—
be she a thing or not a thing,
unriddle now just what she is.

IV.

Diablo

On May 17, 1954, the U.S. Supreme Court ruled in the case of *Brown v. Board of Education of Topeka, Kansas* that state-sanctioned segregation of public schools was unconstitutional.

In September of the same year, on an Air Force base near Salina, Kansas, a young African American teacher was hired to teach a class of twenty white children. That young teacher's daughter, who grew up to become the poet Marilyn Nelson, invited me and several other poets to contribute poems to an anthology dedicated to her mother, imagining the experience through the eyes of a second grader in an all-white classroom, taught by an African American teacher in 1954 on a Kansas military base.

Last year, I was best friends with Marna Dills,
But when her father's term of service ended
Her family left the base and moved upstate
To the big city. Marna sent a card
Last June and said they have a nice house now
And neighbors with a pool they let them use.
She even has a bedroom all her own.
I wrote that I still share with little Hank
And told her how the base had closed the pool
Because it spreads the polio; and then
I asked if she'd been drawing horses lately.

When Marna's family still lived on the base
She used to come to our place all the time
And sit for hours and hours just drawing horses
With pencils and Crayolas at the kitchen
Table, where first, we peeled and sharpened all
The crayons, especially the favorites,
Like Indian Red, Mahogany, and Gold.

Marna could make her horse's legs look real.
Mine looked like sticks. She showed me how to draw
The fetlock joint (her grandpa owns a farm).
She let me copy how she made the hoof
Slant forward like the front end of a train,
The part they call the cowcatcher. Poor cow.
Oh, gosh, I wish you saw the fancy way
She drew her horse's tail and mane in scrolls
Unfurling like a paper party horn
Or birthday streamers flying through the air.

Sometimes she made her horse rear up like Trigger.
She tried to teach me how to draw like her,
But I could never get the hang of it.
We'd draw and draw and hardly talk all day.
My mother'd be in the next room, sipping Sanka
And smoking Lucky Strikes, reading an issue
Of *Photoplay,* and everything felt perfect,
So quiet and good, the way that makes you wish
That nothing ever had to change or end.

I cried a lot when Marna had to move,
And she cried, too. But she came back the time
Her folks drove down to spend Thanksgiving at
Her grandpa's farm. She had a brand new coat
And hat. We sat down at the kitchen table
And started drawing horses just like always.

I watched the shape she made her horse's head
And how the ears tipped up. "Don't copy me,"
She said. "I'm *not,*" I lied, and sneaked a peek.
"I mean it!" Marna leaned across her page
To block my view. "You're such a copycat."
"I'm NOT," I said. All of a sudden, things
Felt different. I sat staring at my clunky,
Unlifelike horse, then thought of an idea,
A trick no one but me would ever think of.
I took the scissors from the drawer and cut
A chunk right off my bangs, while Marna watched
And gasped, "What are you doing?" Then I smeared
My horse's mane and tail with Sanford's paste
And glued my own hair on and smoothed it down.

I made my horse a pinto pony, black
And white, just like Diablo—that's the horse
The Cisco Kid rides on TV. He runs
So fast, he leaves a cloud of dust behind.

Marna said she'd catch holy hell if she
Cut off her bangs like that. She said I'm lucky
My mother has a polio arm so she
Can't spank the way her mother wallops her.

My mother has to lift her polio arm
With her left hand when she salutes the flag;
And how she braids my hair I'll never know.
She doesn't wallop me or little Hank.
If we talk back or don't say "Sir" and "Ma'am,"
The Sergeant takes his belt to us when he
Comes home from duty, and it stings like blazes.
That's why we always do our chores and go
To bed at eight o'clock, no matter what.

Marna has made a lot of friends at her
New school, and some of them are rich. They even
Have swimming pools in their back yards. "Gee, must
Be nice," I said, and peeked at Marna's horse
And how she curved the neck and made the nostril
Curl 'round itself like a backwards number six.
Now that her dad's no longer in the service
And working at the bank, she said, they might
Put in their own pool too, one day. "Gee, must
Be nice," I said again. "Stop saying that.
You sound retarded." She drew more curlicues
And started telling me about her teacher.

"I swear, she's the most boring teacher in
The universe," she said. "But, still, at least
She's *white*. I pity anyone who has
A colored teacher. You poor thing. I thank
My lucky stars we moved." My mother cleared
Her throat from the next room. "You know, Marna,
Just 'cause a person's colored doesn't mean
She can't be a terrific teacher." Marna's
Face made a kind of smirk. "It's true," I said.
"You don't know what you're missing. Mrs. N.
Is really nice." A squeak came out of Marna
The way the mice squeak when the traps go off.
"You're weird," she said and kept on coloring,
Pressing so hard, her crayon cracked and broke.
She put it down and started whispering,
"Remember how you wrote and said they had
To close the pool because of polio?
That isn't what I heard. I heard they closed
The pool because a nigger went in swimming."

My mother slammed the *Photoplay* down hard.
"That pool was polio-closed," she hollered, angry
As all get-out and stormed into the kitchen.
"We don't allow that word inside this house.
You should know better, Marna Dills. And who
Would ever tell you such a shameful lie?"

"The kids at my new school were saying it."
She talked so low, I barely heard her voice.
Her face turned sunburned red, and later on
I didn't mind when Marna had to go.

After she left, my mother stared and squinted
At me and asked what happened to my bangs.
I showed her Diablo's matted mane and tail
Where chunks of hair were glued. She wasn't mad
At all and said she liked Diablo more
Than any horse that Marna ever drew.
"I'd say there's something cruel about the way
Marna draws eyes," she said. It felt like heaven
When she put Diablo in her keepsake drawer.

I set three places at the supper table,
Because the Sergeant would be late again
Down at the NCO club with his buddies.
Then little Hank came in from playing next door.
He said he heard the neighbors say the Sergeant
Cracked up the Ford because he drinked too much.
"He *drank* too much," was all my mother said.
Hank's six years old and dumb as mud. He thinks
Horses will go extinct like dinosaurs,
And that's why I won't ever get to have one.

Tonight, I'll pray to God whose art's in Heaven,
That little Hank is wrong, and one day Mrs. N.
And I can ride the range like Pancho and the Kid,
And leave the bad guys in the dust, the way they did.

"I'll Catch a Ride"

Just days ago, I dropped him off this way
At one of those disorganized, impromptu
Teenage soirees. I offered to come back
Later to pick him up, but mothers should,
As much as possible, remain unseen
For these intensely private, perilous years.
As usual, he said he would get home
Somehow, and so he did, almost on time.

This morning we drive into Forest Lawn.
Again he's vague. I recognize some faces
As he slips out to join his edgy peers,
A clan of gypsies, wearing suits and beads
And shades. They puff their smokes like movie stars,
Embrace like Europeans, some in tears.

It wasn't drugs or gangs or suicide
Or driving recklessly that killed their friend,
Adam, the drummer, at sixteen—but cancer.
Incomprehensible and cruel, I thought
When I was told, and my son's quiet shrug
Spoke loud about the uselessness of words;
So now I watch him learning on his own
Among the monuments and epitaphs.

I'm only in the way, so I move on.
Morning evaporates above the green,
Impeccable, severely watered vistas,
As June gives up its gloom to sudden heat.

Some fool has left a frantic little dog
Alone and yelping in a warming car.
The doors are locked. I think of breaking in.
I hate to leave my son in this strange place,
And wonder how he'll get back home this time.

Stella and Her Bone

How tenderly her tongue
Takes marrow from the bone,
Secured between her paws,
As if to clean her young—
Protected, as her own.
How lovingly she gnaws
And cracks it in her jaws.

A Quiet Evening at Home

The TV station lies about the war.
The wife goes off to bed, stifling a yawn.
The husband trusts the lies and watches more
Inaccurate reports about the war.
It's getting late; the husband starts to snore.
The automatic window shades are drawn.
The TV station lies about the war.
The shares go up. The tax accountants yawn.

Don't Speak to Me of Joy

"This is a war against children,"
said a UNICEF medical doctor in Gaza.

"The president and his team has [sic] been working 24/7 to get to a
 ceasefire,"
said White House spokeswoman Karine Jean-Pierre.

"So many are being killed, it is as if it means nothing,"
said a corpse shrouder in Gaza.

"We will not stop working to achieve a ceasefire deal,"
said President Joseph R. Biden.

"Your taxes are killing us!"
said a Palestinian father to the people of the United States.

"Joe Biden repeats calls for ceasefire,"
said BBC News.

"Don't bother, no one cares,"
said a fleeing citizen of southern Gaza to a photojournalist.

"Defense stocks are attractive investments,"
said U.S. News.

"Nothing remains for the soul,"
said Mosab Abu Toha, a Palestinian poet.

Soldier on the Plane

He could have been a messenger from Mars,
part boy, part man, and part machine of battle,
conspicuous in desert camouflage,
boarding Southwest from Oakland to Seattle.

His earth I.D. read, "U.S. Army Harte."
"Defending Freedom" spanned the copperplate
around his wrist. From boot to crown, clean-cut,
straitlaced, a fledgling ace at brawls of state,

that troop was good to go. The paperback
he opened up was purest raw pulp fiction.
The cover spelled out loud and clear its stark,
impelling title: *Violence of Action.*

He stared into it deeply, as a child
into a jar of tadpoles or a cage
containing well-loved creatures of the wild,
and calmly understood and turned each page—

or so it seemed to me as I observed
his young, decided, stationary face.
A mind's a narrow vault when it's resolved,
and one idea freezes it in place.

I liked to think the pen clipped to his shirt
might serve as Harte's survival gear for wit,
a sidearm to fire questions or assert
some doubt. I wished him luck deploying it.

V.

Autobiographical

October gains as days decrease,
Prompting the orb weaver to spin
What autumn bids it to release
From summer's ripened abdomen.

The Rose in the Center of the Room—A Wedding Toast

For Jesse and Ariel

Let's say two lives are like a house
        And love's their living room,
Where passion blazes on the hearth;
        And say there is a loom

That weaves a rug of intricate
        Design, one of a kind,
To lie on near the fire and feel
        Warm hearts and thoughts entwined.

And at the center, a single rose
        That takes your breath away
Stands fresh and fragrant in its vase
        And never fades away;

Its petals never drop or dry;
        Its colors always stay.
A rose whose fairness lasts forever?
        Impossible, you say?

The budding flower unfurls itself
        Before us, on this day.

"I Almost Just Woke Up"

    For Katarina

My Swedish niece wrote
Me a postcard from Thailand.
The charm of her note

Was how she expressed
Having just woken up, and,
Before getting dressed

Or going outside,
She emerged from her dreaming
Near the early tide

Of a blue-green sea
And a pearly strand of beach,
And she wrote to me,

While the world was caught
Between ambiguities—
Part dream and part not.

May Nasturtiums

Street handsome . . . golden runaway
　　—In memory of Thom Gunn

Their wild, non-native season ends
Before we wish to see them go.
For weeks they graced our car-choked glens
In shimmering, cascading glow—

As one with a capacious heart,
Who reveled in the seediest worlds,
Lifted a grubby vine to art,
And showered the Tenderloin with pearls.

Fair pulse, your bloom is brief, seraphic;
It weaves its unimpeded tropes,
Then leaves us staring at mere traffic,
Winding below the sallow slopes.

Olea Europaea

The salty Peloponnese flood
Of minerals and Trojan blood
Is in this oily, briny fruit,
Savored by Milton to salute
The poets of antiquity.
It is the flavor of the sea
And ink squirtings of cephalopods;
Mortality plucked from the gods'
Martinis at the end of time,
When guilt squares up with every crime,
And joy has run its final course,
And nothing but divine remorse
Attends the last aperitif:
It is the very taste of grief.

The Lesson of the Artichoke

    The buds are harvested before their hour,
Then must be steamed or boiled before they yield
The tongue-like sepals with their toothsome bracts
Attached to the receptacle, or heart,
    That stores the petals of the future flower.

    Your mother will instruct you how to score
Each fleshy leaf between your teeth until
You reach the inmost flimsy purple tent
Tethered above the terminated thistle,
    Which nestles neatly in the meaty core.

    She'll use her knife to sever and excise
The petal-bristles from their concave bed,
Explaining that they're in the way, and that
They're called the choke, and you must never eat them,
    Nor let them keep you from the savory prize.

    Because you know your mother wouldn't trick you,
And life (so far) has not been dangerous,
You dip the gutted heart in melted butter
    And gird your novice tongue for the unknown.
    When you want more, she offers you her own.

"Brightening As They Fail"

>In memory of Anthony Hecht

Autumn's pale foliage comes curtsying down,
As elms release a quiet amber rain.
The punctual sky collects its summer loan
Of blue, and yellow's all that's left of green.
I'm in the habit of a lowered gaze,
Absorbed in nature's horizontal screen,
Askim with fall's ecliptic matinees
Of pas de deux deciduous ballets.

Without exception, each leaf joins its shade
And stops the dance with breathless certainty;
It's what's supposed to happen, after all—
The sombrous kissing game, the mute cascade,
The sun's diminished luminosity,
The shadow creeping up the garden wall.

Forbidding Fruit

Resigned to wheelchair life, too weak to stand,
She cursed her body, calling it a hearse.
The family stopped eating from her hand
The day she put her mortgage in reverse.
Likewise, her mood regressed from bad to worse:
Restricted diet, ill-prepared and bland,
The mortifying mop-ups by the nurse—
She killed a kind word with a reprimand.

Still, fleeting joy could take her by surprise,
As when she bit into that Bartlett pear:
Sweet recognition danced across her eyes,
Glad juice spilled down her cheek into her hair.
She held the bitten fruit out like a prize
That none, not one of them, wanted to share.

White Christmas

I drove my father to the Desert Palms
Medical Plaza where we took a seat
In the air-conditioned waiting room, after
His name was added to the sign-in sheet.

The Epiphany had passed, and still the fake
Tree blinked above the dummy Christmas gifts,
While palm trees decked the parking lot outside
Through windows stencil-sprayed with snowy drifts.

Some plastic evergreens were gathering dust
And fading on the sill. An orchestra
Over the intercom played standard tunes
Of peace on earth and fa la la la la.

While others in the room scrolled at their screens,
We chose a magazine and leafed through news.
Something about a famed comedian's death
Prompted my dad to start in on the Jews.

I'd heard it all before, but even so,
Could not believe my ears. "Jews can't be trusted,"
He said. "They're always favoring their own."
I hid my face, embarrassed and disgusted,

Hoping no one had heard, then flipped the page to
Vacations in Japan, and, as I feared,
He muttered something else about the Japs.
How fitting when an Asian nurse appeared

In fiercely spotless polyester white
To lead my father back to Dr. Stein,
While *Walking in a winter wonderland*
Accompanied the cooling system's whine.

I studied the Potemkin Christmas scene
And almost laughed, because it was so sad:
The polyvinyl greens, the sprayed-on snow,
The empty gifts, good will towards men, my dad.

Happy Hour

> *Now is the night one blue dew, my father has drained,*
> *he has coiled the hose.*
> —James Agee, *A Death in the Family*

My father, if my memory serves me well,
never contended with a hose at dusk,
but chilled Beefeaters as his ritual,
then swirled the pitcher with a marble whisk.

My mother sat across from him and crossed
her dancer's legs, while Perry Como sang
about a falling star. Lamplight caressed
their faces as if nothing could go wrong.

Whether a father drains and coils the hose,
or sips a dry martini with his wife
while crooners from the hi-fi bend a note,
the ease of custom moors him to his days,
holds fast against the ebb and flow of life.
He'll switch to bourbon when his luck runs out.

In Memoriam

Absence

Today the sparrows sing a formal song,
As if they had some tribute to declare;
Wild honeybees imbibe the bright oxalis
And sip the rosemary with gentle care.

A warming softness settles through the garden;
Its sweet lament lingers in every shape.
There's nothing here that will not miss her presence
And nothing that her presence can escape.

Words Spoken, Graveside

   Lake Forest Cemetery, Illinois—April, 2005

We honor these who gave us life:
Father, mother; husband, wife.
May this dear place of final rest
Be ever peaceful, ever blessed.

Song

I'm walking in the footsteps
Of those who came before—
The ones who came before me
And aren't here anymore;
And when I walk on out of here,
I'll leave by the same door.
I'm walking in the footsteps
Of those who came before.

The House Sitter

For weeks I have their places to myself.
I roam their rooms and poke around in drawers,
Peruse the masterpieces on the shelf
(If any), open closets, smoke outdoors,
Lie bare on hand-loomed rugs and parquet floors.

It's Paradise, attending with no care
To other people's temporal domains,
And waken in a disenfranchised glare
Of borrowed sun through someone else's panes,
Indifferent to the clutter of their gains.

And when the moon has gone through several sizes,
I pack, then roll the trashcans to the street.
When they return, my hosts are spared surprises:
No floating koi, no lifeless parakeet,
No philodendrons prostrate from the heat.

I'm incidental to their spoils and waste,
An Eve with no dominion or cachet;
Expelled from Eden without wrath or haste,
I have instructions simple to obey:
'On leaving, strip the bed. Enjoy your stay.'

Clair de Lune

What is this fascination with the moon,
Especially in its fullest, final phase?
It makes a common and inconstant muse,
With borrowed light that gives the palest rays,
Inspiring platitudes and maudlin praise.

It idles in the rangy eucalyptus,
Reclusive in its cool albino gloom;
Then, like a watchman on his graveyard rounds,
Directs its chalky glow into our room,
And Debussy emerges from his tomb.

And then, there is the matter of indifference:
For all our fancying, the moon's a cold
And lifeless satellite. Outweighed and cast
Involuntarily into earth's hold,
It chills to silver sunlight's borrowed gold.

Yet we adore our loyal evening escort.
Despite its flaws, it draws us without trying
And stirs us with its hedonistic wholeness,
Then goes in tactful stages of goodbying,
As if to teach the grace of timely dying.

Doggedness

The sun has followed through and come again
To tint my windowpane pearlescent gray.
It's cloudy, but it isn't going to rain;
That's the official forecast for today.

The fly resumes its angry arabesque;
The child across the street heads off to school;
I gravitate in stages to my desk
And take my swivel throne, summon the fool.

On cue, the neighbor's dog begins to yelp;
Its chambers echo like a catacomb.
I'd go and comfort it, if that would help,
But it's not me it cries for to come home.

The dog is at a loss without its master.
It clamors in confusion at its lot.
You'd think it had been stranded by disaster,
The way it howls. It overrides all thought,

As if a distant dog awaited me
In some abandoned place I knew before;
I'll search for it and keep it company,
Until my own master comes through the door.

Riddle

Arriving here is often an ordeal,
And leaving will most likely be the same.
Some seem to know exactly what to do;
Some wander blindly, wondering why they came.

Though not a place, it's where all things exist,
Except perfection, which no one will find;
And when, at last, the lease is not renewed,
No forwarding address is left behind.

More clues: It starts and ends and has a middle;
The subject is, itself, often a riddle.

Notes

The answer to "The Ultimate Riddle" is a riddle.

The answer to "Riddle" is life.

About the Author

Born in Los Angeles, California, Leslie Monsour was raised in Mexico City, Chicago, and Panama. She is the author of *The Alarming Beauty of the Sky* (Red Hen Press, 2005), *The Colosseum Critical Introduction to Rhina P. Espaillat* (Franciscan University Press, 2021), and several chapbooks, including *The House Sitter* (Finishing Line Press, 2011), winner of the 2010 Finishing Line Press Open Chapbook Competition.

Her poems, essays, and translations appear in such journals as *Able Muse, Alabama Literary Review, The Dark Horse, First Things, Galway Review, Literary Matters, Light, Los Angeles Review of Books, Mezzo Cammin,* and *Poetry,* as well as numerous anthologies ranging from *California Poetry from the Gold Rush to the Present* to *Outer Space: 100 Poems*. Her work has been featured several times on Garrison Keillor's NPR program, *The Writer's Almanac,* as well as Poet Laureate Ted Kooser's syndicated column *American Life in Poetry.*

The recipient of five Pushcart Prize nominations and an NEA Fellowship, Leslie Monsour currently resides in Los Angeles, where she serves as Poet Laureate of Laurel Canyon.

www.ingramcontent.com/pod-product-compliance
Lightning Source LLC
Chambersburg PA
CBHW022015160426